RUBANK EDUCATIONAL LIBRARY No. 41

RUBANK
Elementary
METHOD

SAXOPHONE

N. W. HOVEY

A FUNDAMENTAL COURSE FOR INDIVIDUAL
OR LIKE-INSTRUMENT CLASS INSTRUCTION

HAL•LEONARD®
CORPORATION
7777 W BLUEMOUND RD PO BOX 13819 MILWAUKEE, WI 53213

LESSON 1

Whole Notes and Whole Rests

Half Notes and Half Rests

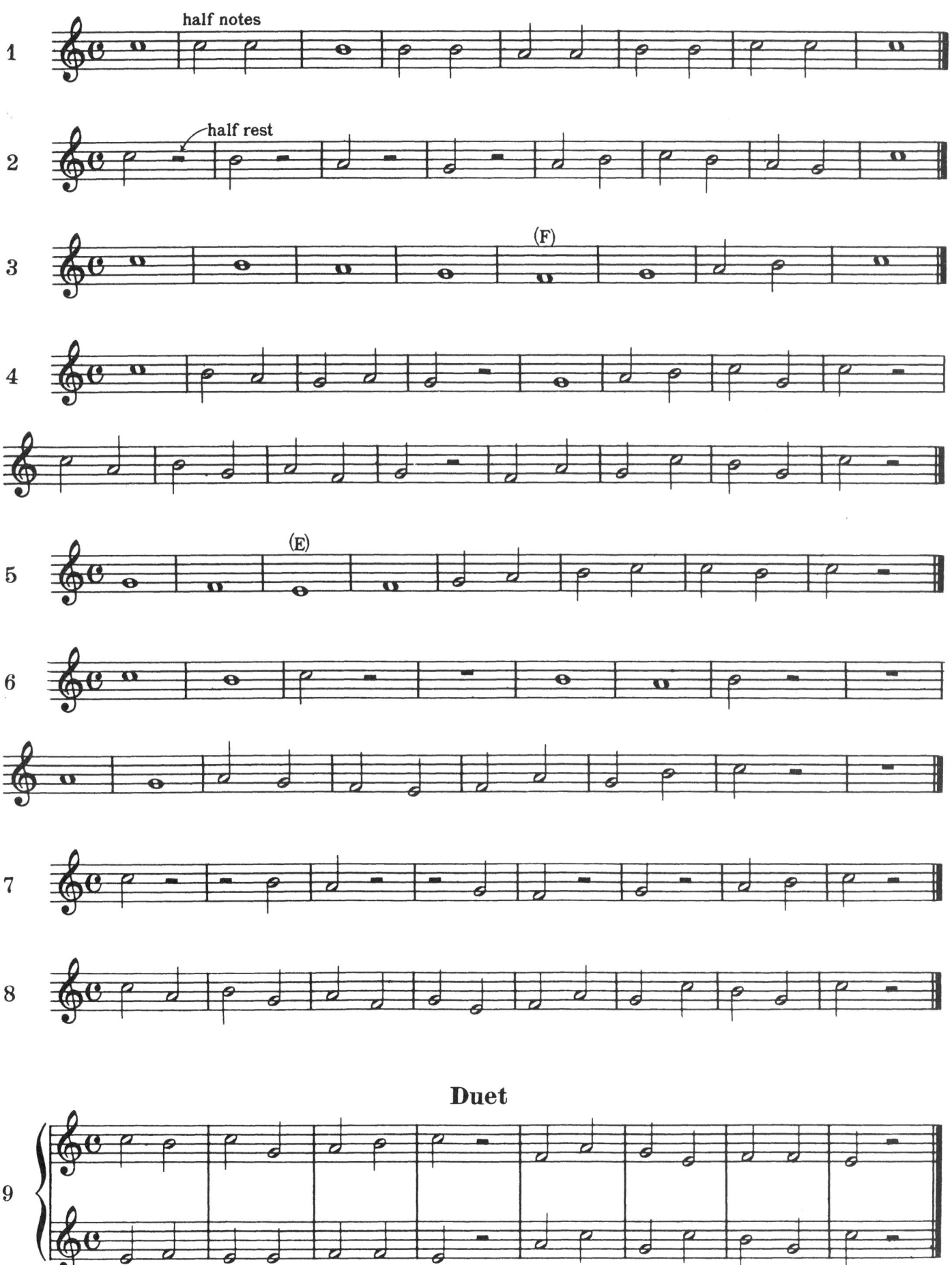

Extending the Range

Also play no. 8 in half notes

etc.

Also play no. 9 in half notes

etc.

Quarter Notes

★) The sign ✗ indicates that the preceding measure is to be repeated.

Rubank Elem. Meth. 392-393

Quarter Notes and Rests

Note: Check the pitch of the high "A" by playing octaves and listening carefully. A slight change in lip tension may be necessary.

Key of F
(one flat — B)
(B♭)

2–4 time; two counts in a measure instead of four.

Duet — Lightly Row

The Tie; Dotted Half Notes

Duet

*) see footnote

*) The sign ♮ is called a "natural". It cancels the effect of the B♭ in the key signature for one measure only. Occasional sharps, flats, or naturals not appearing in the key signature are called accidentals.

Rubank Elem. Meth. 392 - 393

Three Quarter Time

Duet – German Waltz

LESSON 9

Eighth Notes

Rhythmic patterns to be practiced. Repeat each several times.

Duet—Blue Bells of Scotland

Eighth Notes

Duet—Long Long Ago

D.S. is an abbreviation for Dal Segno which means "from the sign." Go back to the sign (𝄋) and play to *Fine* (end).

Slow – sustained – as even as possible in volume and pitch.

Eighth Notes

C major scale
(memorize)

F major scale
(memorize)

Review Lesson
for development of technique
(see footnote)

This page may be given as a single lesson or it may be assigned in parts, according to the ability of the pupil. No new problem is taken up at this point.

Key of G

(one sharp – F)

Duke Street

G major scale
(memorize)

Before proceeding with lesson 14, be certain that you can recognize and define the key signatures that you have had thus far (namely, C, F and G) and that you have *memorized* three major scales.

Dotted Quarter Notes

Rhythmic patterns to be practiced.   Repeat each several times.

Duet—In the Gloaming

A. F. HARRISON

Dotted Quarter Notes

Note time signature.

Slurs

Key of B♭
(two flats—B and E)

Trio to "Ambassador" March

DAVIS

★ Use correct B♭ fingering in major chord.

B♭ major scale (memorize)

Play four major scales from memory before proceeding with lesson 18.

Eighth Rests

Rhythmic patterns to be practiced. Repeat each several times.

Eighth Rests

Alla Breve
(cut time)

Alla Breve

1 *★ see footnote*

2

Alla Breve March

3

4

*★) STACCATO – A dot placed over or under a note (♩♩♩ or ♩♩♩) indicates *short value*. Thus a staccato quarter should be played similar to an eighth note followed by an eighth rest.*

written   played

Rubank Elem. Meth. 392 - 393

Alla Breve

Rhythmic patterns to be practiced. Repeat each several times.

Trio to "Airport" March

EISENBERGER

24

Key of D
(two sharps—F and C)

America, the Beautiful

SAMUEL A. WARD

Six-Eight Rhythms

Practice each of the following 6-8 lessons beating *six* to a measure, emphasizing or slightly accenting counts 1 and 4 (*1 2 3 4 5 6*). Then review each lesson beating *two* to a measure, so that the first beat falls on count *one* and the second beat on count *four*. $\left(\begin{smallmatrix} 1\ 2\ 3\ 4\ 5\ 6 \\ 1\ \text{-}\ \text{-}\ 2\ \text{-}\ \text{-} \end{smallmatrix}\right)$

26

Six-Eight Rhythms

Duet–Drink to Me only with Thine Eyes

English Air

German Folk Song

Six-Eight Rhythms

Duet—Silent Night

GRUBER

Believe Me, If All Those Endearing Young Charms

MOORE

Review Lesson for Development of Technique

Key of E♭

(three flats — B, E, and A)

Exercise on High Notes

Duet — There is a Green Hill

STEBBINS

E♭ major scale
(memorize)

Play six major scales from memory before proceeding with lesson 29.

30

Sixteenth Notes

(see footnote)

Accompaniment Rhythms

Number 1 is a rhythmic exercise. Play both lines and compare. Notice that any eighth note may be replaced by two sixteenths. Invent some rhythmic patterns of

[your own.

Sixteenth Notes

Sixteenth Notes

1

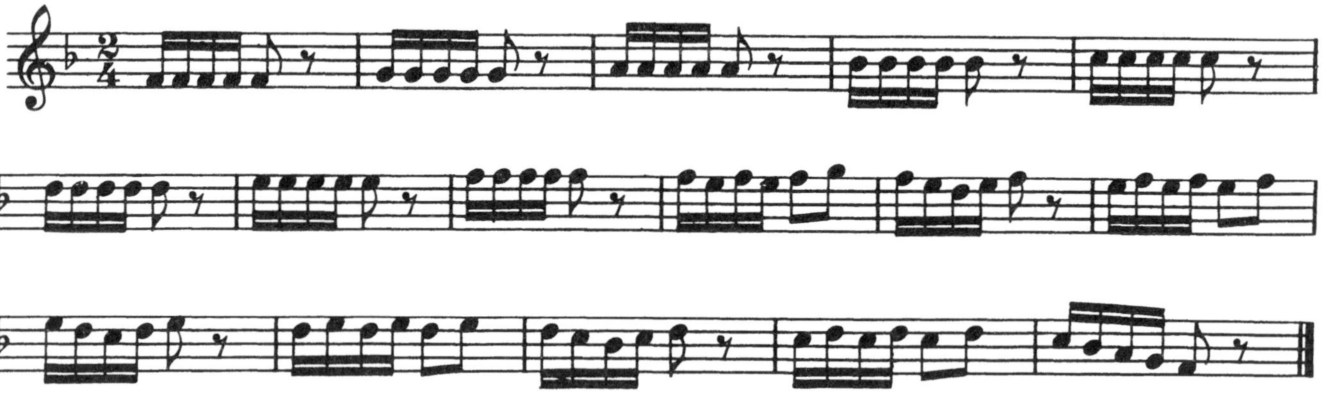

2

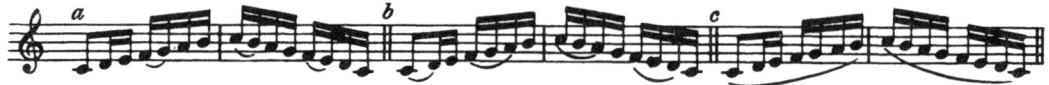

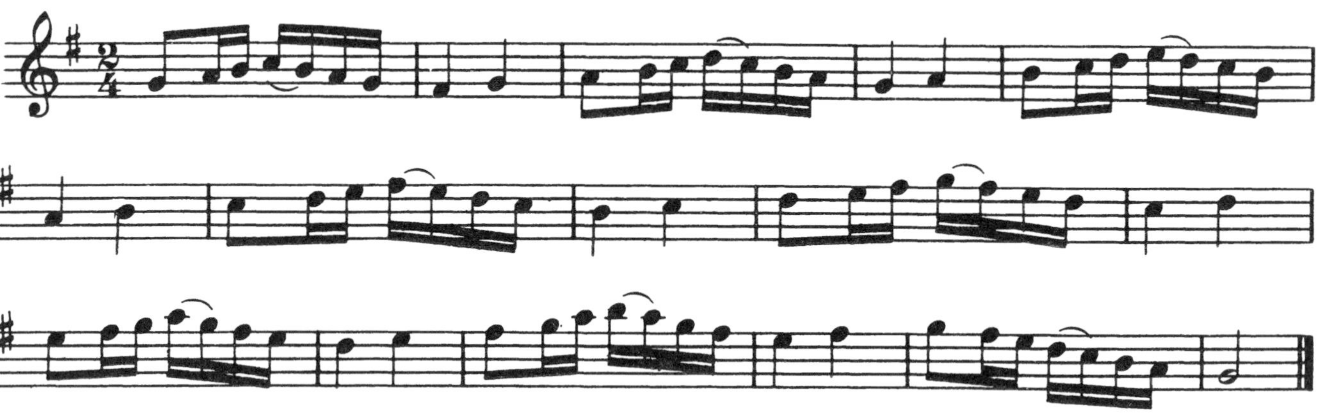

3

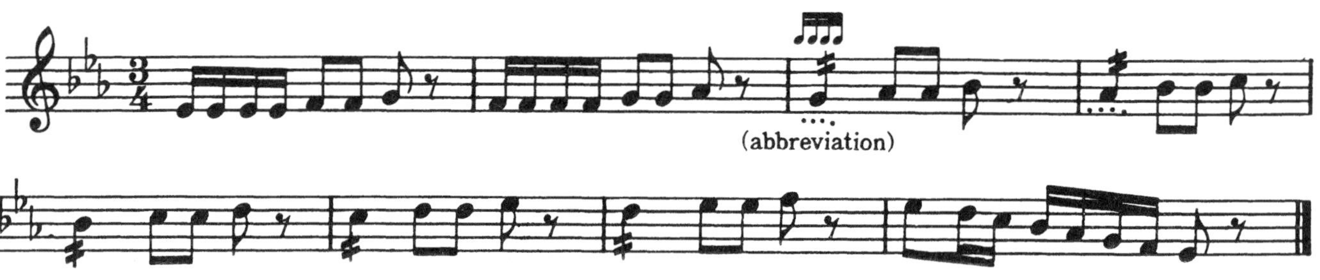

4

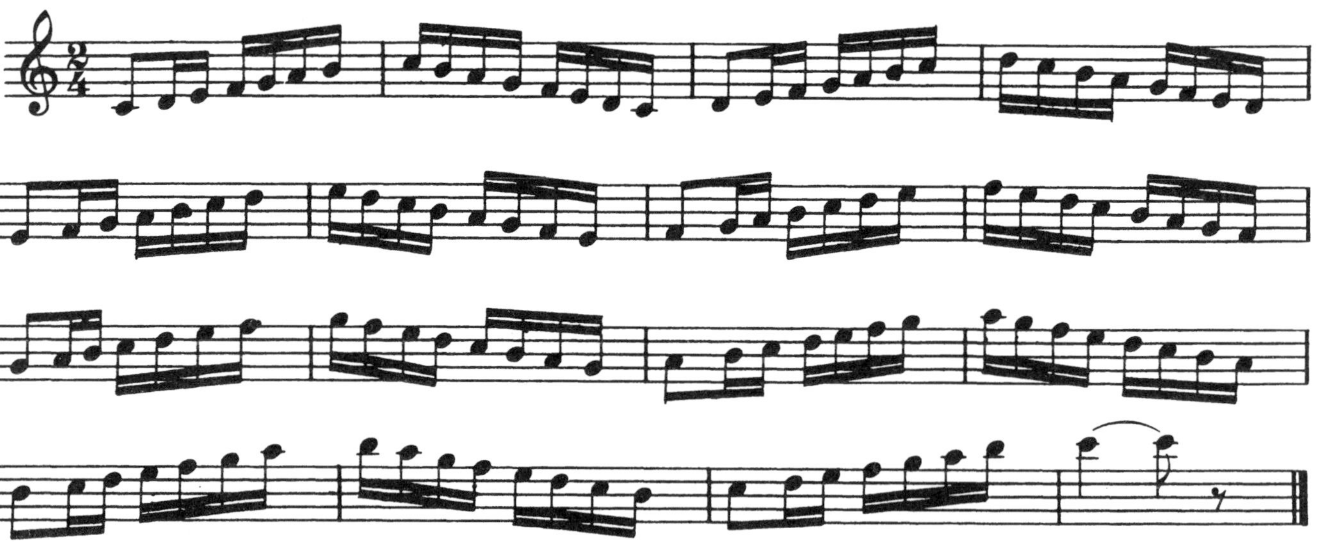

Review no. 4 using these articulations:

Key of A

(three sharps—F, C, and G)

Sweet and Low

BARNBY

A major scale
(memorize)

Play seven major scales from memory before proceeding with lesson 33

Dotted Eighths Followed by Sixteenths

Duet—Tramp, Tramp, Tramp

ROOT

Dotted Eighths Followed by Sixteenths

Trio — My Maryland

Additional Rhythms in Alla Breve

March

Review Lesson for Development of Technique

Key of A♭
(four flats — B E A and D)

Melody

SCHUMANN

A♭ major scale (memorize)

Play eight major scales from memory before proceeding with lesson 38.

Rubank Elem. Meth. 392 - 393

Syncopation

Old Folks at Home

FOSTER

Annie Laurie

Scotch Melody

Be certain the accent is on the correct note.
A common error is committed by playing
syncopated figures as follows:

(incorrect)

tu tu ah tu

Syncopation

Key of E

(four sharps—F, C, G and D)

Technical Study

Hunter's Chorus

WEBER

E major scale (memorize)

Play nine major scales from memory before proceeding with lesson 41.

Chromatic

Chromatic

Waltz

Triplets

In previous lessons you have divided the quarter notes into two equal parts (♩ = ♫) and into four equal parts (♩ = ♬). It may also be divided into three equal parts: (♩ = ♪♪♪).

Scenes That Are Brightest

WALLACE

Be certain you play each of the notes in the triplet figure with equal value. A common error is committed by playing the figure in this way: ♫♩. Do not rush the first two notes.

A Study on Construction of Major and Minor Scales

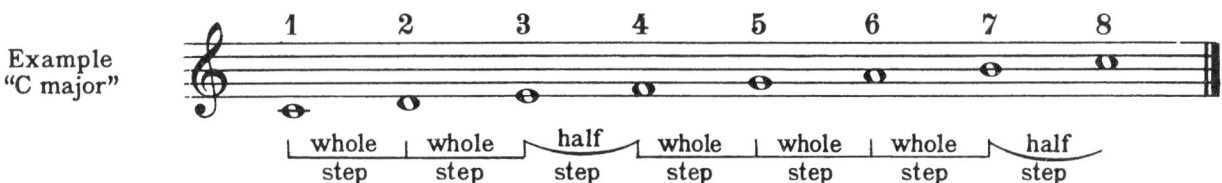

Example
"C major"

To be SPELLED correctly a scale must be on successive lines and spaces. Note HALF STEPS between 3rd and 4th degrees and 7th and 8th degrees.

Work out the following scales, then fill in correct key signature.

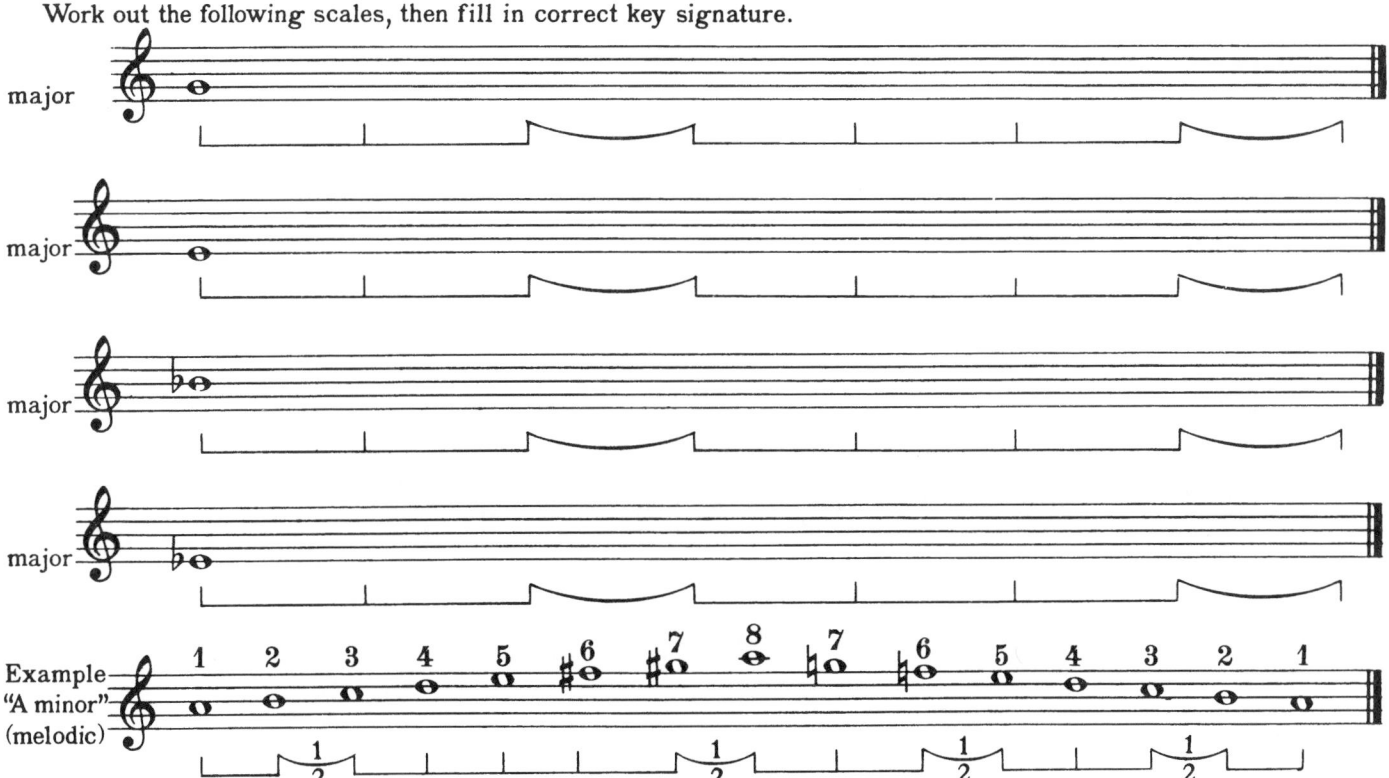

major

major

major

major

Example
"A minor"
(melodic)

Note that the key signature is that of the RELATIVE MAJOR SCALE which starts on the third degree of the minor. In the above example (A minor) the key signature is the same as C major (called the RELATIVE MAJOR) which starts on the third degree of the A minor scale.

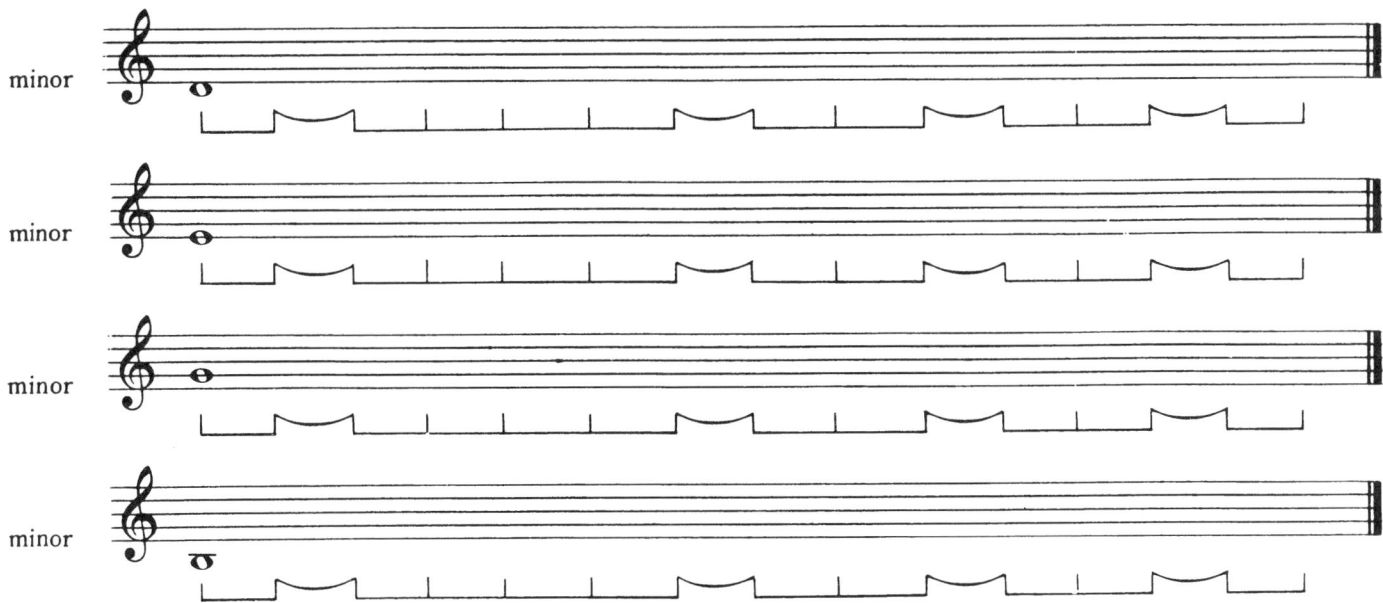

minor

minor

minor

minor

Rubank Elem. Meth. 392-393

Major Scales for Reference

Common Minor Scales

Chromatic

Chord Studies

Tonic _____| Dominant 7th of the new key_____